The Apache Scouts: The History and Legacy of the Native Scouts Used During the Indian Wars

By Sean McLachlan & Charles River Editors

Apache scouts at Fort Apache, Arizona in the 1880s

About Charles River Editors

Charles River Editors provides superior editing and original writing services across the digital publishing industry, with the expertise to create digital content for publishers across a vast range of subject matter. In addition to providing original digital content for third party publishers, we also republish civilization's greatest literary works, bringing them to new generations of readers via ebooks.

Sign up here to receive updates about free books as we publish them, and visit Our Kindle Author Page to browse today's free promotions and our most recently published Kindle titles.

About the Author

Sean McLachlan has spent much of his life in Arizona and Missouri, working as an archaeologist and tracing legends of the Old West. Now a full-time writer, he's the author of many history books and novels, including *A Fine Likeness*, a Civil War novel with a touch of the weird. For more information, check out his Amazon page and blog.

Introduction

Apache scouts in the 1870s

The Apache Scouts

"Even if we should be able to dislodge them from the rough mountain ridges and impenetrable woods which cover the immense territories of these frontiers, they would seek better asylum in the vastness of the Sierra Madre... [They] know how to surprise and destroy our troops in the mountains and on the plains. They are not ignorant of the use and power of our arms; they manage their own with dexterity; and they are as good or better horsemen than the Spaniards, and having no towns, castles, or temples to defend they may only be attacked in their dispersed and movable rancherias." - Bernardo de Galvez, *Instructions for Governing the Interior Provinces of New Spain, 1787* (The Quivera Society, Berkeley)

The Apache of the American Southwest have achieved almost legendary status for their fierceness and their tenacity in fighting the U.S. Army. Names like Nana, Cochise, and

Geronimo are synonymous with bravery and daring, and the tribe had that reputation long before the Americans arrived. Indeed, among all the Native American tribes, the Spanish, Mexicans, and Americans learned the hard way that the warriors of the Apache were perhaps the fiercest in North America. Based in the Southwest, the Apache fought all three in Mexico and the American Southwest, engaging in seasonal raids for so many centuries that the Apache struck fear into the hearts of all their neighbors.

First migrating to the Southwest from western Canada sometime around 1000-1500, the Apache lived a hunting and gathering lifestyle in the rough mountains and vast stretches of desert left unused by the agricultural peoples who had preceded them, or fought for the scarce temperate highlands of the region's many mountain ranges. The Apache kept herds of animals and would trade and raid with the settled tribes.

Successive waves of immigrations would change Apache lifestyle forever. First the Spanish and then the Mexicans moved into what is now northern Mexico, Arizona, New Mexico, and western Texas. The newcomers were few at first, but even so, the Apache felt the pinch as they were pushed out of some of their traditional grazing and hunting lands. More serious trouble began in the mid-19th century with the conquest of the region by the United States and the influx of large numbers of ranchers, farmers, and miners. The Apache were soon cornered into the most remote areas and conflict became inevitable.

The U.S. Cavalry bore the main burden of pacifying the region and found it incredibly difficult to track down the Apache, who had an intimate knowledge of the terrain and could disappear into the rough mountains without leaving more than a trace of their passing. The cavalry tried many different tactics, including hiring native scouts, but it wasn't until they hired Apaches to go after other Apaches that they were able to finally defeat the hostile bands.

The story of the Apache scouts is one of the most unusual in the annals of military history, a tale of a supposedly superior army adapting the strategy and tactics of a much smaller and technologically inferior foe. Like the majority of Native American groups, the Apache were eventually vanquished and displaced by America's westward push, but the Apache's military prowess remain legendary.

The Apache Scouts: The History and Legacy of the U.S. Army Indian Scouts Used in the Apache Wars analyzes the use of native scouts and the history of the Apache wars that stretched over decades. Along with pictures of important people, places, and events, you will learn about the Apache scouts like never before, in no time at all.

The Apache Scouts: The History and Legacy of the Native Scouts Used During the Indian Wars
About Charles River Editors
About the Author
Introduction
   Chapter 1: The Origins of the Apache
   Chapter 2: Early Experiments with Apache Scouts
   Chapter 3: An American Problem
   Chapter 4: Organizing the Apache Scouts
   Chapter 5: Apache Scouts In Action
   Chapter 6: Rebellion at Cibecue Creek
   Chapter 7: The Apache Kid
   Chapter 8: The Final Era
   Online Resources
   Bibliography

Chapter 1: The Origins of the Apache

While the origin of the name "Apache" is a point of contention among modern linguists, many believe it was derived from the Yavapai word epache, meaning "people," while also having some relationship with the Zuni word *apachu*, meaning "enemy." Another popular assertion is that "Apache" was actually the Zuni designation for the Navajo and not specifically the Apache people, because early Spanish chroniclers wrote that the Zuni name for Navajo was "Apachis de Nabaju," with "Apache" actually a Quechan word meaning "fighting-men. Today, the Apache prefer the designations *N'de, Dišnë, Tišndende, Inde,* or *Nide* (meaning "the people.")

The most widely-accepted hypothesis dates the arrival of the Apache, Navajo, and Ute to around 1500, during what is referred to as the "Dinétah" archaeological phase of the Upper San Juan River drainage area in northwestern New Mexico, southwestern Colorado, southeastern Utah, and northeastern Arizona. Another common theory contends that these groups first entered the U. S. Southwest during the Historic period after the Puebloan Revolt of 1680, when the Pueblo nations expelled Spanish colonizers and restored self-rule. Yet another theory, which is promoted by Barry Pritzker in *Native American Encyclopedia: History, Culture, and Peoples*, is that Athabaskan ancestors of the Apache and Navajo migrated into the Southwest around 1400, but physical evidence does not support this contention yet. Whatever the timing, historians consider the Apache, Navajo and Ute as relative "new arrivals" to the region, and they arrived as hunter-gatherers, establishing villages north and between Anasazi, Mogollon, and Hohokam homelands. By some reckoning, both the Apache and Navajo constitute subgroups of the Ute people, with the Apache infiltrating the Southwest and establishing themselves in the Great Basin. Other historians contend that the Ute actually arrived in the Southwest as early as 1200 and were responsible for driving out the Puebloans virtually single-handedly.

While these theories trace the Apache migration from Northwestern Canada (and perhaps Alaska) to the Southwest around 1500, some Apache groups contend that it actually occurred in reverse. They contend that around 1500 and contact with the Spanish, most Athapaskan-speaking people migrated to the north, with only a minority remaining in the Southwest. Whichever direction they came from, everyone agrees that by the end of the 1600s, about 5,000 Apache occupied the Southwest.

Once the Apache, Navajo and Ute separated from the Athabaskan-speaking group in Canada, the Apache-Navajo migrated south along the High Plains of the United States, following the outer ridge of the Rocky Mountains and passing through Montana and Nebraska. Encountering comparatively more-aggressive Plains groups like the Pawnee along the way, who at this time lived in fortified villages and conducted small-scale farming, the Apache remained more mobile, while the Navajo adopted basic farming techniques. Upon arrival in the Puebloan homelands, the Apache and Navajo began to experiment with farming, settling pueblo-like villages (building *hogans,* permanent wooden and stone structures) and raiding surrounding Puebloan settlements.

It was this activity that presumably resulted in the exodus by the remaining Anasazi, Mogollon, and Hohokam.

When those groups left, the Navajo and Apache essentially divided up the Southwest territory, with the Navajo assuming control of the "Four-Corners" area and the Apache taking the mountains and plains of southern Arizona and New Mexico and northwestern Mexico. It was from there that the Apache eventually subdivided into the Arivaipa, Chiricahua, Coyotero, Faraone Gileno, Llanero, Mescalero, Mimbreno, Naisha, Tchikun, and Tchishi subgroups, but they were collectively known as a powerful and warlike people.

Chapter 2: Early Experiments with Apache Scouts

Although the Spanish didn't formally mention the Apache until 1598, when Spanish Conquistador Don Juan de Oñate y Salazar entered the region, historians think it likely that Spanish explorer Francisco Vásquez de Coronado was referring to the Querecho Apache in 1541 when he described a group he encountered on the Plains of east New Mexico and west Texas. Coronado wrote, "After seventeen days of travel, I came upon a 'rancheria' of the Indians who follow these cattle. These natives are called Querechos. They do not cultivate the land, but eat raw meat and drink the blood of the cattle they kill. They dress in the skins of the cattle, with which all the people in this land clothe themselves, and they have very well-constructed tents, made with tanned and greased cowhides, in which they live and which they take along as they follow the cattle. They have dogs which they load to carry their tents, poles, and belongings."

Regardless of when they encountered the Apache, the Spaniards colonized the upper Rio Grande Valley by 1598, bringing large numbers of livestock and horses to the West and Southwest. Almost immediately, the Spanish drive northward disrupted traditional Apache trade with neighboring tribes and alerted them to possible invasion. The Apache had been trading with the Pueblo and also stealing from them during raids, and once the Pueblo began to acquire horses, the Apache quickly began taking horses and adopting Spanish cavalry tactics. Crafting leather shields and chestplates, they armed themselves with Spanish-style lances (in addition to their traditional bows and arrows) and were quickly able to assume military dominance of the region. With superior numbers the key to their former battle strategies (and one reason most Apache groups never subdivided into small bands), the Apache could now take on considerably larger forces regardless of numerical disparities. Thus, by 1650, the so-called "horse frontier" was regarded by most as "Apache Territory" and was strictly avoided unless the people entering the region were prepared for confrontation.

The Apache came to the attention of the Spanish military when they started raiding in the 1650s and then aided the great Pueblo Revolt of 1680, which for a few years pushed the Spanish out of the region. By 1710 they were making frequent and serious raids into Spanish territory, and by 1750 threatening to push the Spaniards out a second time. Settlers in outposts such as Tubac (founded 1752) and Tucson (founded 1769) cowered behind town walls at night, and were under threat whenever they ventured forth to tend their herds and fields.

It is during the early Spanish period that the Apache first encountered wild horses and for a time considered them game. At some point the Apache developed their own riding style that differed from the Spanish style, so it seems they did not learn riding from the colonists but rather by independent invention. Reports from the Pueblo Revolt of 1680 showed that the Apache had already become excellent horsemen by this early date. While the Apache adopted some elements of Spanish culture, most particularly metalworking, their traditional method of fighting was what gave them the upper hand. The Spanish were not sufficiently willing or able to adapt their fighting to the circumstances and paid the price.

In fact, the Americans weren't the first to use Native Americans as scouts in the Southwest. As the Spanish struggled to defeat hostile tribes, especially the Apache, they hit upon the idea of asking friendly tribesmen for help. By the 1790s, the Spanish had organized a native militia made up of mostly Pima Indians from what is now southern Arizona and had equipped them with guns. They also employed small numbers of Apache scouts, although it appears they didn't trust these fierce warriors with firearms. Records are sparse, but their efforts clearly helped reopen the trade route between Sonora and the northern frontier of what is now Arizona and New Mexico, which had been cut off by hostile Apaches a century earlier.

This worked until 1810, when supplies dried up thanks to the economic and political deterioration of the Spanish Empire in the wake of the Napoleonic Wars. Sensing the Spanish were weak, the Apaches and other tribes rose up to regain their lands. By the time Mexico achieved independence in 1821, the region had been all but lost to Hispanic settlement. The Mexicans started putting more pressure on the region in the ensuing decades but their control was tenuous at the best of times.

The Mexican government was loathe to employ native scouts, although they did use some from the Pima, Yavapai, and other cooperative tribes. The Apache and the Mexicans, however, were mortal enemies, and no Apache would fight for them. The governments of Sonora and Chihuahua placed bounties on Apache scalps, including children's scalps, and roving gangs of scalp hunters would descend on Apache settlements and kill everyone there. Small towns would often trick the Apaches into thinking they were friendly, ply them with alcohol, and then ambush them when they were intoxicated. Geronimo himself almost died in one such ambush. Sometimes Apache women and children weren't killed for their scalps but were instead sold into slavery in the mines or large *haciendas*.

Geronimo

Chapter 3: An American Problem

In 1848, a victorious United States forced Mexico to sign the Treaty of Guadalupe Hidalgo, ending the Mexican-American war. The United States gained 525,000 square miles of land, including California, New Mexico, Arizona, Nevada, Utah, and parts of Wyoming and Colorado. A key section of the treaty read, "Considering that a great part of the territories, which, by the present treaty, are to be comprehended for the future within the limits of the United States, is now occupied by savage tribes, who will hereafter be under the exclusive control of the Government of the United States, and whose incursions within the territory of Mexico would be prejudicial in the extreme, it is solemnly agreed that all such incursions shall be forcibly restrained by the Government of the United States whensoever this may be necessary; and that when they cannot be prevented, they shall be punished by the said Government, and satisfaction for the same shall be exacted all in the same way, and with equal diligence and energy, as if the same incursions were meditated or committed within its own territory, against its own citizens."

When the United States took over Arizona and New Mexico in 1848 after the Mexican-American War, at first the Apaches were friendly. The Americans had defeated the hated Mexicans, after all, and seemed open to trade. Soon too many whites came, however, and tensions rose. Another factor was gold prospecting. The Apache thought of gold as holy. It was the only metal that wasn't, in their view, useful for anything and thus belonged to the god Ussen. To dig it up was considered sacrilege and the cause of earthquakes and other natural disasters.

The influx of whites into New Mexico Territory (what is now New Mexico and Arizona) in the 1850s led to a decline of game and available rangeland. Skirmishes between settlers and Apaches became common and some citizens groups took matters into their own hands and set out parties to hunt them down. Soon, relations descended into open hostility, and tensions escalated in December 1860 when a group of miners launched an unprovoked attack on an Apache rancheria.

This provoked the famous war chief Mangas Coloradas to start his long fight against the settlers. Mangas Coloradas, was well known to the Americans, having made a treaty with them as far back as 1852. At that time, the war leader was known for his bitter raids across the border into Mexico. During the 1852 negotiations, Mangas was asked why he continued to fight against the Mexicans while making terms with the Americans. He replied, "I will tell you. Some time ago my people were invited to a feast; aguardiente, or whiskey, was there; my people drank and became intoxicated, and were lying asleep, when a party of Mexicans came in and beat out their brains with clubs. At another time a trader was sent among us from Chihuahua. While innocently engaged in trading. . .a cannon concealed behind the goods was fired upon my people, and quite a number were killed. . .How can we make a peace with such a people!" Mangas was captured in 1863, and as the soldiers camped that night with their prize, they tortured him and then allowed him the chance to run so they could claim they had "shot him while trying to escape." He suffered the indignity of having his head cut off, boiled to remove the skin, and sent east for "scientific" examination by the phrenologist Orson Squire Fowler. There could be no worse fate for an Apache; in the Apache afterlife, called Happy Land or Cloud Land, the spirits of the dead existed in the form in which they were buried, so mutilation was considered a fate worse than death. At the same time, the Apache saw such acts as proof that they were fighting barbarians.

From the 1840s-1860s, the American Southwest was sorely undermanned. The American army was small and not enough troops were sent to protect the frontier. The U.S. Army was stretched thin, with only a few scattered forts manned mostly by Dragoons armed with single-shot muskets and almost no artillery. These Dragoons roved through the desert and mountains of the Southwest, chasing after bands of hostile Apache and other tribes. While they had some success, the natives knew the land far better than they did and found it easy to disappear into the deep canyons and rough mountains and elude pursuit.

Travelers or those who lived outside of the few remote settlements found themselves vulnerable, so civilians tried to fight back by forming ad hoc militias. These tended to be amateurish outfits that rarely caught up with any hostile Apaches. If they did, it was usually an unguarded rancheria where the vigilantes descended on the women and children and then rode back to the nearest saloon to boast of their martial prowess.

A notable exception were the vigilante groups organized by King Woolsey, an early rancher and prospector in Arizona who once mixed pinole with strychnine and gave it to a group of Indians just to watch them die. Woolsey led three major operations against Apaches through some of the roughest terrain in the region. Woolsey hated the Apaches but also understood them. After fighting off a raiding group at his ranch on the Gila River about 80 miles north of Yuma, he hung the body of an Apache he had killed on a tree as a warning to others, thus playing on the Apache's fear of dead bodies. Woolsey's ranch was left unmolested after that.

King Woolsey

For his raids, Woolsey recruited large groups of well-armed and mounted civilians along with pack animals and brought back loot and scalps. One interesting note from Woolsey himself in 1864 was that he discovered the Tonto and Pinal Apache were making arrows in the style of the Mohave and Yavapai, hoping to fool the whites into thinking those generally friendly tribes were doing the raiding. Woolsey is also notable for his early advocacy of using Indians, including Apaches, as scouts.

In one expedition in 1864, Woolsey led about 40 men, including a band of 14 Maricopa Indians, after a band of Apache that had been stealing cattle. The party penetrated the deep gorge of the Salt River where few white men had ever been, and about 35 miles in they spotted a group of Apache warriors further up the side of the steep canyon. There appeared to be about 250 of them.

A standoff ensued, and while the Apaches were stripped and painted for war, it seems they did not come out intending to fight the party (otherwise the whites wouldn't have seen them until they fired). Both sides hid behind rocks and called out to each other in Spanish, and eventually it was decided to meet halfway and parlay. Woolsey told his men that if he touched his hat with his left hand, they were to open fire. He then set out with four others of his party and met six of the Apaches part way up the slope. Both sides went apparently unarmed. In fact, the whites concealed pistols under their coats. It's doubtful the Apaches could have concealed much since they were wearing only breechclouts, although one trailed along a spear behind him.

The two parties sat down together on an outspread blanket and talked through Woolsey's translator, while Woolsey told each of his friends in English who to shoot when the fighting started. Once each man had his assignment, Woolsey touched his hat. There was a roar of pistols, and five of the six Apache delegates fell over. The sixth man, the one with the spear, took a mortal injury but had strength enough left in him to skewer one of the treacherous whites. The rest of Woolsey's party charged up the gorge, firing on the remaining Apaches, and there was a brief firefight before the Apaches fled. Woolsey's party suffered several wounded and the Apaches lost about a dozen more men.

In other expeditions, Woolsey used small numbers of Apache scouts to great effect. It may seem surprising that Apaches would attack their own people, but it must be remembered that there was little sense of unity in Apache culture. While such a sense would increase in the face of ever-greater incursions by the Americans, Apaches were (and remain) a fiercely independent people. Chiefs had only limited power and relied on their greater experience and charisma to keep the people in their band in line. War chiefs were simply the most experienced warriors. No one, in peace or wartime, had to obey a chief if they didn't want to. People could always leave a band, and war parties were made up of volunteers only. These war parties were generally made up of warriors from the war chief's own band, with a few other warriors from friendly bands coming along for the sake of filial loyalty and the chance for loot.

Groups of Apaches also warred with each other, especially if they were from different regions. This was used advantageously by the famed Indian fighter Kit Carson in a raid against the Comanche and Kiowa-Apache in 1864, during which he used numerous Jicarilla Apache scouts. Carson's raid was launched from New Mexico to stop Comanche and Kiowa-Apache incursions from the Texas Panhandle. The Kiowa-Apache lived in the Southern Plains area and had become acculturated to Plains Indian ways. They traditionally raided further south and thus the Jicarilla thought of them as "bad neighbors."

Carson

The Civil War was in full swing, and the frontier forts were even more undermanned than usual as soldiers had been recalled to fight the major battles in the East. Various tribes took advantage of this to raid settlements and try to regain lost land, and both the Union and the Confederacy encouraged the tribes to raid each other's territory. The Comanche and Kiowa-Apache living in the Texas Panhandle raided both the Confederate regions of Texas as well as Union areas of Colorado and New Mexico.

Kit Carson, who at that time was a colonel in the Union army in New Mexico, led 335 troops and 75 Ute and Jicarilla Apache scouts out to punish the Comanche and Kiowa-Apache. The soldiers marched about 250 miles across almost empty wilderness from Fort Bascom in New Mexico to Adobe Walls in northern Texas. Adobe Walls was an old trading post, abandoned in

1845 but still a notable landmark in the north Texas flatlands. The scouts were essential for guiding the column there and protecting its flanks. They were also responsible for spotting several Comanche and Kiowa-Apache winter camps, and in the early hours of November 25, Col. Carson led his men into battle.

Carson soon found he had bitten off a bit more than he could chew, and his small command had to fend off wave after wave of hundreds of warriors, whose ranks only grew as more of their comrades from nearby villages rode in to join the fight. The Kiowa-Apache warriors at first put up a stiff resistance to allow their women and children to escape, and then withdrew to await reinforcements from the other camps. The line of battle reached the old ruins of Adobe Walls, with good visibility on all sides, and here the troops decided to make their stand.

At first the artillery kept the Kiowa-Apache and Comanche at a distance, but as their numbers swelled to a thousand, they grew bolder. Some continued riding back and forth in front of the troops, firing from behind their horses. Others crept up through the grass to snipe at the soldiers. While Carson's men held them off, they were taking casualties (including one unfortunate fellow who was bitten by a snake when lying on the ground) while the Indians' numbers only increased.

While the Ute and Jicarilla Apache scouts could have run away from this dangerous situation, they remained in the thick of the fight. As the artillery officer Lt. George Pettis noted, "Our Indians, mounted and covered with paint and feathers, were charging backwards and forwards and shouting their war cry, and in their front were about two hundred Comanches and Kiowas, equipped as they themselves were, charging in the same manner, with their bodies thrown over the sides of their horses, at a full run, and shooting occasionally under their horses' necks, while the main body of the enemy, numbering twelve or fourteen hundred, with a dozen or more chiefs riding up and down their line haranguing them, seemed to be preparing for a desperate charge on our forces. Surgeon Courtright had prepared a corner of the Adobe Walls for a hospital, and was busy, with his assistants, in attending to the wants of half a dozen or more wounded. Fortunately, the Adobe Walls were high enough to protect all our horses from the enemy's rifles, and afford ample protection to our wounded."

During a lull in the fighting, Carson ordered a withdrawal. The battle was essentially a draw, with the Comanche and Kiowa-Apache retaining the field while Carson's force gave them a bloody nose deep in their territory and burned one of their villages. The native scouts had proven their ability, as Kit Carson, who understood Native American culture well, knew they would.

Chapter 4: Organizing the Apache Scouts

The end of the Civil War led to a boom in immigration to the Southwest and further encroachment on traditional Apache hunting and gathering grounds. The postwar army was stretched thin and had trouble scouting in the vast deserts and rough mountains, many of which hadn't even been adequately mapped. Civilians, especially newspaper editors, constantly complained that not enough was being done to solve the Indian problem, while at the same time exacerbating that problem by encouraging the hunting down of Indians. Many times, local citizens groups would find an Apache rancheria and burn it to cinders, killing anyone they could catch.

Apache retribution was equally heartless. On 26 May 1870, a wagon train of merchandise left Tucson heading for Camp Grant, 55 miles to the northeast. The wagon train was owned and led by High Kennedy and Newton Israel and included several women and children. They never made it. A group of some 50 or 60 Apaches descended on the wagons and killed all the men, carrying off the women and children. One of the officers from Camp Grant, Captain John Bourke, described the scene when he got there: "There were hot embers of the new wagons, the scattered fragments of broken boxes, barrels, one or two broken rifles, torn and burned clothing. There lay all that was mortal of poor Israel, stripped of clothing, a small piece cut from the crown of the head, but thrown back upon the corpse—the Apaches do not care much for scalping—his heart cut out, but also thrown back near the corpse, which had been dragged to the fire of the burning wagons and partly consumed; a lance wound in the back one or two arrow wounds, a severe contusion under the left eye, where he had been hit perhaps with the stock of a rifle or carbine, and the death wound from ear to ear, through which the brain had oozed. The face was as calm and resolute in death as Israel had been in life."

During the late 1860s and early 1870s, the U.S. Cavalry used a great many Indian and Mexican scouts. The Mexicans could be relied upon to eagerly chase the Apache, whom they hated, but they often killed the Apaches indiscriminately. Indian scouts such as the Pima and the Navajo were found lacking as well; while they knew the terrain, they also feared the Apache's skill in warfare, to the extent that many officers became convinced their Indian scouts were steering them the wrong way to avoid fighting.

The army used a few Apache scouts in this period, but not with any consistency or regularity. There was no official policy to hire Apache scouts, so it was up to the initiative of the individual commanders. One early Apache scout was Manuel Duran, employed by the experienced Indian fighter Lt. Howard Cushing. Cushing also hired Joe Felmer, who was not an Apache himself but was married to one and knew their language and their ways. Felmer is recorded to have given the soldiers this nugget of frontier wisdom: "When you see Apache 'sign', be *keerful*; 'n' when you don' see nary sign, be *more* keerful."

Early successes demonstrated to the army that Apache scouts could be trusted. In 1863 and 1864, the undermanned frontier army in Arizona had to fight the rebellious Navajo, who decided that now that the white men were fighting each other, they could reassert their independence. In 1863. In response, the army started hiring Apache scouts to fight them because the Apache had a long tradition of raiding the Navajo for their crops and knew the approaches to their remote settlements well. The Apache proved excellent at tracking down Navajo raiding parties and climbing the sides of almost impassable canyons in northern Arizona and New Mexico to get to where the Navajo lived. It was not until after the Navajo were defeated that Congress approved Native Americans to be officially enlisted in the army in July 1866.

The 1870s were the worst time for both sides in the Apache Wars. The Apaches suffered relentless incursions into their lands during the wave of westward migration after the Civil War, and many peaceful Apache bands were persecuted. The worst single incident happened in April 1871 and became known as the Camp Grant Massacre. A group of Tucson vigilantes and some Pima Indians raided a peaceful reservation of Pinal and Aravaipa Apaches near town and slaughtered about 150 of them. Several of the women were assaulted before being killed, and most of the victims, including small children, were scalped.

This barbaric behavior convinced many Apache to respond in kind. Settlers suffered from frequent Apache raids, and soldiers rode themselves ragged trying to catch the raiders, more often than not ending up getting ambushed along the way.

Matters did not improve until the arrival in 1871 of a new commander for the region: Lieutenant Colonel (later General) George Crook. Crook came to Arizona with a distinguished military career fighting Indians and Confederates. He was, by all accounts, sober, humble, and willing to listen to those who knew the local area better than he. While he was fully prepared to defeat the Apache militarily, he was also sympathetic to the needs of those who wanted peace.

General Crook

Once he was in Tucson, he wasted no time. He called in officers from all parts of the Arizona Territory and grilled them about conditions on the ground. Then he set out to hunt down Cochise and other hostile Apaches. He hired Mexican scouts for their knowledge of the land and their willingness to fight, but soon became dissatisfied with them. They often ignored commands from lower-grade officers and failed to discriminate between friendly and hostile Apaches. Having suffered from years of Apache depredations, the Mexicans wanted to eliminate all Apaches. Revenge was more important than discipline.

Then Crook hit on the idea of using Indian scouts. Whether or not he knew of the Spanish experiments of the previous century is unclear, but to his astute mind the advantages were obvious; they knew the land better than anyone, were expert trackers, spoke the language, and could tell friend from foe. At first he hired Pima and Navajo. While they proved better than the Mexicans, local commanders complained that they were reluctant to fight. Some even accused the scouts of leading the U.S. Cavalry away from the Apache in order to avoid contact.

Finally Crook decided to take a gamble by hiring Apaches to hunt Apaches. While this seemed a bad idea to some, Crook understood Apache culture better than any other high-ranking officer in the West. It is common practice to look upon "inferior" or "native" cultures as a monolithic people, thinking in lockstep with one another, but Crook saw beyond that and understood that Apaches were highly individualistic, their scattered bands having little formal leadership and looking out for their own interests. It was easy to find settled Apaches eager to take regular pay to fight fellow Apaches.

It also helped relieve discontent on the reservations that were being set up for the Apaches. The various Apache bands were being forced onto bad land and told to farm. Corrupt reservation officials sold many of the rations earmarked for them, and gave them inferior tools with which to cultivate the land. Farming was traditionally women's work and the young warriors felt humiliated at being forced to till the soil. Many leapt at the chance to prove themselves as fighters, even if it was for the white man. One Apache account by James Kaywaykla, who grew up in this time and fought in Victorio's band, reflects the Apache attitude towards the scouts. "Ours was a race of fighting men—war was our occupation. A rifle was our most cherished possession. And though the scouts were permitted to have only five bullets at a time, and to account for each one fired, a weapon is a weapon. And, believe me, there was not a man who did not envy the scout his rifle."

Victorio

General Crook knew this instinctively, and often offered renegade Apaches he had just tracked down and defeated the chance to join his scout companies. He saw that the wilder an Apache was, the better scout he would make, and his long list of successes proved him right. Apache scouts signed on for a six-month service, which was later extended. An Apache who signed up for less than six months had to supply his own horse and equipment, and at first, they were issued with a Civil War surplus uniforms and weapons. In battle they tended to discard the uniform and fight Apache fashion, wearing only the traditional loincloth and moccasin boots, plus a red bandanna so that their white comrades wouldn't shoot them by mistake.

The first scouts were mustered into the army and ready for campaigning by November 1872. Apache scouts generally signed on for a six-month service, a period that was later extended. An Apache who signed up for less than six months had to supply his own horse and equipment. At first, scouts were issued with a Civil War surplus uniforms and weapons. In battle they tended to discard the uniform and fight Apache fashion, wearing only the traditional loincloth and moccasin boots, plus a red bandanna so that their white comrades wouldn't shoot them by mistake. They valued the uniforms, however, because it was fashionable for Apaches to sport

American or Mexican clothing when not engaged in fighting.

Success was instantaneous. Crook tirelessly hunted down hostile bands and the Apache scouts proved expert at leading him to them. There were problems, however. While Apache scouts were relatively free of the strict discipline regular soldiers endured, they were still placed in an ordered regime alien to them. Disagreements and misunderstandings often arose over their terms of stay. In a traditional Apache raiding party, an individual could leave at any time. This, of course, was not allowed in the U.S. Cavalry.

Another problem was that of personal vendettas. Some Apaches signed up as scouts to settle scores with personal enemies. This proved a problem if the army wanted to bring back prisoners. If sent against groups with whom they had sympathy, they sometimes led the cavalry astray or warned their friends of the cavalry's intentions, or least that's what their white commanders accused them of doing.

Many Apache saw these scouts as traitors. For example, the Chiricahua scout Chato, or Flat Nose, who was well-respected by cavalry officers and even headed the delegation to Washington to discuss the removal of Apaches to the East in 1886, had a bad reputation among many Apaches. He was considered a brute and a bully, but his unpardonable sin was aligning himself with the U.S. Cavalry under false circumstances. He had joined in 1883 after a failed bid to become an Apache war leader. Chato was soon first sergeant of Company B, Apache Scouts under the command of 2nd Lt. Britton Davis, despite there being many more experienced scouts in the unit. The Apaches claimed he had Mickey Free, another scout and "coyote" (renegade), translate falsely in order to make Chato look good and to hurt the reputation of respected leaders such as Geronimo and Chihuahua. Mickey Free told Davis that the two leaders were trying to kill him.

Crook was pleased with developments but remained convinced that those Apache that had not already settled onto reservations would have to be forced to do so. The year 1872 had seen many raids by "wild" Apache, and parts of the Arizona Territory were all but uninhabitable for whites and Mexicans. Thus, he launched an offensive in November 1872, the goal of which was to eradicate the defeat the numerous bands of hostile Apaches and force them onto reservations once and for all. He sent out several columns into the areas of eastern Arizona where resistance was at its height, with the goal of attacking the rancherias and driving the Apaches into the snow-capped mountains, where privation would eventually force them to submit to government authority. Each column was well supplied with Apache scouts as well as mule trains and packers. This latter element of the campaign was an innovation of Crook's. Earlier campaigns had all too often relied on cumbersome supply wagons that were slow on good ground and useless in the mountains. Some commanders had tried mules before, but Crook hired the best packers in the territory to ensure that the operation ran efficiently.

Despite these troubles, hiring Apaches as scouts proved to be a resounding success, and many soldiers later admitted they could have never defeated the renegade Apaches without them. General Crook stated, "I cannot too strongly assert that there has never been any success in operations against these Indians, unless Indian scouts were used. These Chiricahua scouts…were of more value in hunting down and compelling the surrender of the renegades than all other troops…combined. The use of Indian scouts was dictated by the soundest of military policy."

The renegades agreed with this sentiment as well. James Kaywaykla, who rode with Victorio, later said, "it was the scouts whom the Apaches dreaded, for only they knew the trails and the hiding places. And only they could traverse the country rapidly enough to be a menace."

Chapter 5: Apache Scouts In Action

Scout companies were made up of 25 men commanded by a white officer. At the height of the campaigns of 1877 and 1878, there were some 600 Apache scouts mustered into the army. By the time of the relatively more peaceful years of 1885-1886, when the army was hunting Geronimo but most other renegades had been caught, the number had dropped to 200.

When not chasing renegades, the scouts generally lived on the reservation fort with their families. While there, they performed garrison duty and also kept an eye on their fellow tribesmen. They weren't the only ones. A Chiricahua Apache named Sam Kenoi recalled that many Apache were secretly on the payroll: "At Fort Apache they said Geronimo was always suspicious. There were two women and three men who were secret service agents for Lieutenant Davis. They were Western Apache. These are a different tribe. That is what caused many of the stories that were going around. The two women who were secret service agents would go after midnight to these army officials and tell them what had been said, what the Indians intended to do. Most of the trouble came through the Western Apache. They told stories, mostly false. We don't know who the secret service people were. But I don't think the government officials can deny that they had secret agents, men and women."

The constant campaigning ensured the scouts didn't stay on the reservation very long. When on the march, the scouts generally roved 12 to 24 hours ahead of the main column, with instructions to locate any hostile Apaches and report back to the soldiers. Being Apaches, however, they were eager for battle and often all the fighting was done by the time the main force of soldiers arrived. Doubts about the scouts' willingness and ability to fight soon vanished, at least among the soldiers. The civilian press took much longer to convince and were always quick to find fault with any particular campaign or battle. If they couldn't find fault, they often made it up.

Even so, the press slowly began to come around as the scouts' record of successes grew longer, and American soldiers in the West knew better. For example, Captain John Bourke wrote of them, "The longer we knew the Apache scouts, the better we liked them. They were wilder and more suspicious than the Pimas and Maricopas, but far more reliable, and endowed with a greater amount of courage and daring. I have never known an officer whose experience entitled his opinion to the slightest consideration, who did not believe as I do on this subject."

Bourke spent many years in the Southwest campaigning against the hostile Apache, and like General Crook he found their culture fascinating. He learned a great deal about Apache ways and later in life became an academic authority on their culture and history. He left several valuable works on the Apache Wars and the Apache people. His book *Apache Campaign* gives a vivid account of working alongside the Apache scouts:

> "A few words in regard to the peculiar methods of the Apaches in marching and conducting themselves while on a campaign may not be out of place. To veterans of the campaigns of the Civil War familiar with the compact formations of the cavalry and infantry of the Army of the Potomac, the loose, straggling methods of the Apache scouts would appear startling, and yet no soldier would fail to apprehend at a glance that the Apache was the perfect, the ideal, scout of the whole world. When Lieutenant Gatewood, the officer in command, gave the short, jerky order, *Ugashe* "Go!", the Apaches started as if shot from a gun, and in a minute or less had covered a space of one hundred yards front, which distance rapidly widened as they advanced, at a rough, shambling walk…

> "They moved with no semblance of regularity; individual fancy alone governed. Here was a clump of three; not far off two more, and scattered in every point of the compass, singly or in clusters, were these indefatigable scouts, with vision as keen as a hawk's, tread as untiring and as stealthy as the panther's, and ears so sensitive that nothing escapes them. An artist, possibly, would object to many of them as undersized, but in all other respects they would satisfy every requirement of anatomical criticism. Their chests were broad, deep, and full; shoulders perfectly straight; limbs well-proportioned, strong, and muscular, without a suggestion of undue heaviness; hands and feet small and taper but wiry; heads well-shaped, and countenances often lit up with a pleasant, goodnatured expression, which would be more constant, perhaps, were it not for the savage, untamed cast imparted by the loose, disheveled, gypsy locks of raven black, held away from the face by a broad, flat band of scarlet cloth. Their eyes were bright, clear, and bold, frequently expressive of the greatest good-humor and satisfaction. Uniforms had been issued, but were donned upon ceremonial occasions only. On the present march each wore a loosely fitting shirt of red, white, or gray stuff, generally of calico, in some gaudy figure, but not infrequently the sombre article of woollen raiment issued to white soldiers. This came down outside a pair of loose cotton drawers, reaching to the moccasins. The moccasins are the most important articles of Apache apparel. In a fight or on a long march they will discard all else, but under any and every circumstance will retain the moccasins. These had been freshly made before leaving Willcox. The Indian to be fitted stands erect upon the ground while a companion

traces with a sharp knife the outlines of the sole of his foot upon a piece of rawhide. The legging is made of soft buckskin, attached to the foot and reaching to mid-thigh. For convenience in marching, it is allowed to hang in folds below the knee. The raw-hide sole is prolonged beyond the great toe, and turned upward in a shield, which protects from cactus and sharp stones. A leather belt encircling the waist holds forty rounds of metallic cartridges, and also keeps in place the regulation blue blouse and pantaloons, which are worn upon the person only when the Indian scout is anxious to 'paralyze' the frontier towns or military posts by a display of all his finery.

"The other trappings of these savage auxiliaries are a Springfield breech-loading rifle, army pattern, a canteen full of water, a butcher knife, an awl in leather case, a pair of tweezers, and a tag. The awl is used for sewing moccasins or work of that kind. With the tweezers the Apache young man carefully picks out each and every hair appearing upon his face. The tag marks his place in the tribe, and is in reality nothing more or less than a revival of a plan adopted during the war of the rebellion for the identification of soldiers belonging to the different corps and divisions. Each male Indian at the San Carlos [Reservation] is tagged and numbered, and a descriptive list, corresponding to the tag kept, with a full recital of all his physical peculiarities.

"This is the equipment of each and every scout; but there are many, especially the more pious and influential, who carry besides, strapped at the waist, little buckskin bags of Hoddentin, or sacred meal, with which to offer morning and evening sacrifice to the sun or other deity. Others, again, are provided with amulets of lightning-riven twigs, pieces of quartz crystal, petrified wood, concretionary sandstone, galena, or chalchihuitls, or fetiches representing some of their countless planetary gods or Kan, which are regarded as the 'dead medicine' for frustrating the designs of the enemy or warding off arrows and bullets in the heat of action. And a few are happy in the possession of priceless sashes and shirts of buck skin, upon which are emblazoned the signs of the sun, moon, lightning, rainbow, hail, fire, the water-beetle, butterfly, snake, centipede, and other powers to which they may appeal for aid in the hour of distress.

"The Apache is an eminently religious person, and the more deviltry he plans the more pronounced does his piety become.

"The rate of speed attained by the Apaches in marching is about an even four miles an hour on foot, or not quite fast enough to make a horse trot. They keep this up for about fifteen miles, at the end of which distance, if water be encountered and no enemy be sighted, they congregate in bands of from ten to fifteen each, hide in some convenient ravine, sit down, smoke cigarettes, chat and joke, and stretch out in the sunlight."

While Bourke says the scouts acted without the usual army discipline on the march, their eyes were alert for any sign of hostile forces, and when they sensed they were getting close to their quarry they would turn serious.

"The scouts became more and more vigilant and the 'medicine-men' more and more devotional. When camp was made the high peaks were immediately picketed, and all the approaches carefully examined. Fires were allowed only in rare cases, and in positions affording absolute concealment. Before going to bed the scouts were careful to fortify themselves in such a manner that surprise was simply impossible."

Other officers also made some interesting observations about the scouts. First Lieutenant Augustin Gabriel Tassin commanded the scouts at Fort Huachuca in 1879. In that year he had an odd double assignment: lead his White Mountain Apache scouts after the renegade chief Juh, while also working freelance for the Smithsonian Institution to write an illustrated report on the flora and fauna of Arizona. He noted:

"All the scouts paint their faces while on the march with red ocker [ochre], deer's blood, or the juice of roasted mescal, for the double purpose of protecting them from the wind and sun, as well as distinctive ornamentation. The ornamentation is a matter of taste and tribal obligation. The other part of the operation is one of necessity, for it is a well-known fact that dirt and grease protect the skin against inclement weather. An Indian seldom washes unless he can grease himself afterwards; and with him in many instances grease takes the place of clothing, for he knows the necessity of an equality of the activity of the skin and the calls upon it, and why, when exposure is very great, the pores should be defended."

"...My scouts were occupied in pre- paring their beds for the night. Grass was pulled by handfuls, laid upon the ground, and covered with one blanket, another serving as cover. They generally sleep with their feet pointed towards little fires, which they claim are warm, while the big ones built by the white soldiers are so hot that they drive people away from them, and besides, attract the attention of a lurking enemy.

"All this time scouts are posted on knolls commanding every possible line of approach. The Apache dreads surprise. It is his own private mode of destroying an enemy, and knowing what he himself can do, he ascribes to his foe—no matter how insignificant may be his numbers—the same daring, recklessness, agility, and subtlety possessed by himself."

The Apache scouts performed some of their best service in an intense period of campaigning from November 1872 to April 1873, when Crook sent out several company-sized columns accompanied by Apache scouts to hunt down the scattered renegade bands. To keep them in the field for longer and make them more mobile, wagons were dispensed with and replaced by mule trains and expert packers. This allowed the columns to chase the hostile Apaches into the most remote mountain retreats, once known only to them but now known to the army as well thanks to their new scouts.

Of course, that didn't make the campaigning any easier. The renegades fought bitterly, inflicting large numbers of casualties on both civilians and soldiers. For the troops, the hard marches over rugged terrain under a punishing desert sun, the climbs up near vertical mountain passes, and the endless skirmishes against an all but invisible foe took a toll on men and equipment. When a weary column returned to the fort for one of its rare breaks, the men would be literally in rags. They would be missing several of their mounts and mules, victims of falls or enemy gunfire, and usually came with sad tales of dead comrades.

Crook pushed his men hard. He sensed the Apache would never give up unless forced to see the hopelessness of their situation, so he set out to prove to them it was hopeless. It paid off as the renegades took losses, both in the countless skirmishes and in major battles such as Salt River Cave in December 1872 and Turret Mountain in March 1873.

At the first battle, also called the Skeleton Cave Massacre, a group of 220 men, including 30 Apache scouts, tracked a band of renegades deep into the Salt River Canyon, Arizona. Their chief, Nanni-chaddi, had hidden in Skeleton Cave, a deep cave on the side of the canyon. Nanni-chaddi had boasted that no soldier had ever found it. The Apache scouts found it, though, and when the Apaches refused to surrender they and the soldiers arrayed themselves below the cave and opened fire. For a while it appeared to be a standoff, until the soldiers and scouts started firing at the roof of the cave, just visible from their positions below. The bullets ricocheted around the cave interior. Several soldiers made it up to the overhanging bluffs and fired down on any Apache who tried to escape, and even rolled boulders down on the defenders.

The fire from the cave lessened and finally died out, and eventually the soldiers charged up the steep canyon and found a scene of terrible slaughter. A total of 76 Apaches had been killed, including chief Nanni-chaddi and many women and children. The 18 survivors, mostly wounded and lying helpless on heaps of their dead, were taken prisoner. Only one soldier died in the fight.

Another resounding victory occurred at Turret Peak on March 27, 1873. Once again the renegades were in an easily defended position, a steep mesa in central Arizona, but the Apache scouts led a group of soldiers up it at night and then positioned them near the Apache camp. As sunlight broke on the top of the mesa, the soldiers and scouts attacked, taking the camp completely by surprise and killing 57 Apaches without taking any casualties. Some of the Apaches were so shocked at this attack that they ran over the edge of the cliff and plunged to their death.

Being a people composed of small bands, any death was a serious blow both psychologically and economically. Every member of the band was necessary for its survival, and taking such heavy losses demoralized the renegades and convinced many to surrender. By the middle of 1873, most of the renegade bands had turned themselves in, having learned that Crook was good to his word of honoring the rights of those who surrendered. They were settled on reservations around Fort Apache and San Carlos, and Crook was rewarded for his work by being promoted to brigadier-general.

Throughout the rest of that year and the next, Crook kept up the pressure against a dwindling number of renegade bands, mostly of the Western Apache. This second offensive was also successful, with Victorio and his band finally negotiating a return to their lands in Ojo Caliente, and the old warrior Cochise dying, remarkably, of natural causes after three decades of fighting Mexicans and Americans.

Now that the situation was calming down, the government made a foolish move. To cut the costs of having so many reservations, they decided to concentrate all the Apache at San Carlos. However, the land there wasn't as good as at some of the other reservations, and it broke the promises given to several chiefs. It also forced several mutually hostile bands to live side by side.

In May 1877, the Ojo Caliente reservation was closed and the Apaches there forced to move to San Carlos. That September, Victorio, Loco, and Nana all led their warriors in a breakout. In a single stroke, bureaucrats in Washington had undone many of Crook's accomplishments. Loco eventually returned, but the other two chiefs continued their fight, leading the army on an exhausting chase through Arizona and northern Mexico.

The Apache scouts continued to chase him and wear down his band. The memoirs of James Kaywaykla, who was with Victorio for much of this time, indicate the band's increasing desperation and defiance. He noted the exhaustion, the hunger, the fear, and also the determination of the dwindling band: "It was a hard life, but we liked it better than the hopeless stagnation of the reservation…Again we had hope for freedom. Hardships imposed on people are much more onerous than those they voluntarily assume."

Victorio, with a last remnant of diehards, fled to Mexico, where he was finally cornered by some 400 Mexican soldiers and killed at Tres Castillos in October of 1880. That left only Nana, the aged warrior who had seen 75 years of conflict. He gathered together the survivors of Tres Castillos and some of his own people and struck back. In July and August of 1881 he marched some 1,500 miles through New Mexico in six weeks, slaughtering and looting as he went and brushing aside seven army detachments. On his exultant return to the Sierra Madre in September, he was joined by the war chief Juh and a contingent of Chiricahuas, who had fled the San Carlos reservation.

Nana

The renegades returned to San Carlos the following April, but not to surrender. Instead, they all but kidnapped Chief Loco and a band of 400 mostly Warm Springs Apache and made them come with them on the warpath. Going after them were the U.S. Cavalry and a large contingent of Apache scouts, who doggedly pursued them and killed about a hundred before the renegades reached the safety of the Sierra Madre.

Chief Loco

There followed a year of relative calm, but General Crook knew there would never be peace while the renegades remained in the Sierra Madre. Gaining permission from the Mexican government to march through its territory, Crook led a force made up mostly of Apache scouts into the rough mountain range and was able to negotiate a peace. The dispersed bands began to trickle back to San Carlos one by one over the following months, with Geronimo being the last in February of 1884.

Following the death of Cochise in 1874, Geronimo rose to a position of leadership among the Chiricahua Apache, and a few years later, he would earn recognition as one of the most skilled guerrilla fighters in American history. Though Geronimo neglects to mention it in his autobiography, he was part of a group of Chiricahuas from several different bands who spent much of 1882 raiding in Chihuahua and the southwestern United States. In 1883, Geronimo and the other Chiricahuas returned to Mexico and spent over a year in the mountains, likely raiding and stealing. Again the Chiricahuas operated like a guerilla army without the political end goal, living off of the land and the populace. As was their practice, they avoided direct conflict with Mexican troops but engaged them in numerous small actions. In response to an increased Mexican military presence in the mountains, the Chiricahuas returned to Arizona in 1884, hoping to recruit additional warriors to the cause of successful raiding in the mountains of northern Mexico. Unfortunately for the Chiricahuas, they had a conflict of some kind with U.S. troops and lost fifteen warriors. At least, that is the way Geronimo describes the actions of the Chiricahua bands after returning to Arizona. Other sources say the Bedonkohe and members of other Chiricahua bands surrendered and were taken to the San Carlos Indian Reservation.

Geronimo's 1885 escape from the San Carlos Indian Reservation marked the start of his final campaign, and ten months after leaving the reservation, Geronimo and his followers would surrender to U.S. troops in Mexico. Geronimo entered this surrender probably because he trusted the man accepting his surrender, General George R. Crook, a veteran of Phil Sheridan's Shenandoah Valley Campaign in 1864. The Apache had nicknamed Crook "Nantan Lupan," meaning Grey Wolf, and the General had earned a reputation for honesty among the Plains tribes while he served as the commander of the District of the Platte. However, as the small group of Native Americans marched north toward the border escorted by U.S. troops, Geronimo and a group of about 35 other Chiricahuas slipped away, fearing they'd be murdered. Two weeks later, there were reports that Geronimo and his group had massacred a family near Silver City, and that one girl was hanged from a meat hook jammed under the base of her skull. Whether the story was true or not, it certainly created a great deal of apprehension in the region.

When Geronimo and his diehard followers fled the reservation again, General Crook resigned, protesting that meddling by the government and sharp dealing by reservation officials made pacifying the Apaches impossible. The Apaches valued honesty and valued General Crook for being an honest man, but Crook kept having his promises broken for him by government officials.

10 days later, one of the most hardened American veterans of the Indian Wars, General Nelson A. Miles, arrived in the territory, assumed command, and proceeded to change the tactics being used to find and capture Geronimo. Crook's replacement had already enjoyed success in pursuing and capturing Native American leaders and their followers, having force-marched across Montana with his troops in 1877 to capture Chief Joseph of the Nez Perce tribe. In that campaign, the Nez Perce led U.S. troops on a chase that covered over 1,000 miles.

Nelson Miles

Miles drastically diminished the role played by Native American troops – the Apache Scouts – in the effort to find and capture Geronimo, and he quickly deployed some 5,500 U.S. troops in new roles. Some troops were assigned to active patrolling and conducting search and destroy operations in Mexico searching for the Chiricahuas. Additionally, Miles assigned troops to guard all known water holes in the arid region.

Despite this massive effort, which had U.S. troops in pursuit of Geronimo traveling over 1,500 miles, Miles was no closer to finding and capturing the small Chiricahua band three months later. Miles' problems were explained by Bourke's book *On the Border with Crook*, another detailed look at the Apache Wars that offered a great deal of firsthand information about the renegades and the scouts. It contains many passages about the Apache way of war that show just how difficult it was for soldiers to catch Apaches without help from other Apaches.

> "The Apache was in no sense a coward. He knew his business, and played his cards to suit himself. He never lost a shot, and never lost a warrior in a fight where a brisk run across the nearest ridge would save his life and exhaust the heavily clad soldier who endeavored to catch him. Apaches in groups of two and three, and even individual Apaches, were wont to steal in close to the military posts and ranches,

and hide behind some sheltering rock, or upon the summit of some conveniently situated hill, and there remain for days, scanning the movements of the Americans below, and waiting for a chance to stampede a herd, or kill a herder or two, or 'jump' a wagon-train.

"They knew how to disguise themselves so thoroughly that one might almost step upon a warrior thus occupied before he could detect his presence. Stripped naked, with head and shoulders wrapped up in a bundle of yucca shoots or 'sacaton' grass, and with body rubbed over with the clay or sand along which it wriggled as sinuously and as venomously as the rattler itself, the Apache could and did approach to within ear-shot of the whites, and even entered the enclosures of the military camps, as at Grant and Crittenden, where we on several occasions discovered his foot-prints alongside the 'ollas,' or water-jars."

"...The expertness of the Apache in all that relates to tracking either man or beast over the rocky heights, or across the interminable sandy wastes of the region in which he makes his home, has been an occasion of astonishment to all Caucasians who have had the slightest acquaintance with him. He will follow through grass, over sand or rock, or through the chapparal of scrub oak, up and down the flanks of the steepest ridges, traces so faint that to the keenest-eyed American they do not appear at all. Conversely, he is fiendishly dexterous in the skill with which he conceals his own line of march when a pursuing enemy is to be thrown off the track. No serpent can surpass him in cunning ; he will dodge and twist and bend in all directions, boxing the compass, doubling like a fox, scattering his party the moment a piece of rocky ground is reached over which it would, under the best circumstances, be difficult to follow. Instead of moving in file, his party will here break into skirmishing order, covering a broad space and diverging at the most unexpected moment from the primitive direction, and not perhaps reuniting for miles. Pursuit is retarded and very frequently baffled. The pursuers must hold on to the trail, or all is lost. There must be no guess work. Following a trail is like being on a ship: so long as one is on shipboard, he is all right; but if he once go overboard, he is all wrong. So with a trail: to be a mile away from it is fully as bad as being fifty, if it be not found again. In the meantime the Apache raiders, who know full well that the pursuit must slacken for a while, have reunited at some designated hill, or near some spring or water 'tank,' and are pushing across the high mountains as fast as legs harder than leather can carry them."

Bourke also explained in detail how Crook had wisely offered alternatives to fighting, trying to give the Apaches a fair deal and hope for the future.

"Crook's promise to provide a ready cash market for everything the Apaches could raise was nobly kept. To begin with, the enlistment of a force of scouts who were paid the same salary as white soldiers, and at the same periods with them, introduced among the Apaches a small, but efficient, working capital. Unaccustomed to money, the men, after receiving their first pay, spent much of it foolishly for candy and other trivial things. Nothing was said about that; they were to be made to understand that the money paid them was their own to spend or to save as they pleased, and to supply as much enjoyment as they could extract from it. But, immediately after pay-day, General Crook went among the Apaches on the several reservations and made inquiries of each one of the principal chiefs what results had come to their wives and families from this new source of wealth. He explained that money could be made to grow just as an acorn would grow into the oak; that by spending it foolishly, the Apaches treated it just as they did the acorn which they trod under foot; but by investing their money in California horses and sheep, they would be gaining more money all the time they slept, and by the time their children had attained maturity the hills would be dotted with herds of horses and flocks of sheep. Then they would be rich like the white men; then they could travel about and see the world; then they would not be dependent upon the Great Father for supplies, but would have for themselves and their families all the food they could eat, and would have much to sell."

Eventually, Miles had to reassess his strategy, and he decided to send an officer with a small party into Mexico to find Geronimo and negotiate a surrender. The new strategy required General Miles to choose an officer from among those remaining from General Crook's command, because none of his men were familiar with the Chiricahua or spoke their language.

Miles settled on Lieutenant Charles B. Gatewood. A graduate of the United States Military Academy at West Point in 1877, Charles Gatewood had been assigned to the 6th Cavalry Regiment stationed at Fort Wingate, New Mexico. After a year of service at Fort Wingate, the young officer was assigned to command companies of Apache and Navajo scouts in Apache country throughout the southwest. Applying an unusually modern approach and style while serving as the leader of Native American scout companies, Gatewood believed that his best chance for success with the Apache and Navajo troops would come by understanding their culture and attitudes and gaining their acceptance.

The Chiricahua called Gatewood "Baychendaysen" ("Long Nose")

In an effort to achieve these goals, Gatewood met with his troops daily, dismissed ideas of his own racial superiority, and avoided talking down to his Native American soldiers. Lieutenant Gatewood appeared to have a promising Army career ahead of him, but in 1884, he arrested a territorial judge for fraud committed against his Native American wards. General Crook asked Gatewood to drop the charges against the Judge but the Lieutenant refused, and the ensuing litigation eventually made it impossible for Crook and Gatewood to work together.

General Miles' plan involved sending two Chiricahua Apaches whom the U.S. commander considered "friendly," Kayitah and Martine, to carry a message to Geronimo. The two men would be accompanied on the mission by Lieutenant Gatewood and were chosen because both were related to members of Geronimo's party. Gatewood would carry written orders from General Miles authorizing him to requisition any assistance he might need to complete his mission from U.S. military units operating in the field, and the General forbade Gatewood from approaching the Chiricahuas without an escort of at least 25 troops. Gatewood was allowed to pick other team members and recruited interpreter George Wratten and packer Frank Huston to accompany him into Mexico.

After tracking the Apache chief and his followers for several weeks over hundreds of miles, Geronimo eventually attempted to negotiate with Gatewood, but the Lieutenant said he was only ordered to deliver the General's message and had no authority to negotiate terms. The Chiricahuas retreated a bit and discussed the matter among themselves, apart from the soldiers. It being midday, the participants ate lunch and afterwards resumed their discussions. Geronimo then entered into a long listing of the wrongs suffered by his people at the hands of whites and concluded by saying that expecting the Chiricahuas to give up everything to a bunch of intruders was too much. They were willing to give up all of their former territory except the reservation, demanding that Gatewood allow them to return to the reservation or fight. Gatewood repeated his inability to negotiate terms, saying he couldn't take them to the reservation and he couldn't fight with them.

It was decided that the formal surrender would occur in Skeleton Canyon, about 60 miles south of Fort Bowie in the Arizona Territory, and a couple of days later the entire force began moving north towards the U.S. border. After the first day's travel, Aguirre and his force of about 200 Mexican troops approached the U.S. camp and demanded that the Chiricahuas be handed over to the Mexicans for "punishment." Lawton refused, but at Aguirre's insistence, a meeting between a small group of Mexicans and the Chiricahuas was arranged.

By managing to evade thousands of American and Mexican troops for about a year, Geronimo had turned himself into a legendary, almost mythical figure whose name struck fear in the hearts of white settlers across the Southwest. Even then, settlers were referring to him as "the worst Indian who ever lived." His group also represented one of the last groups of Native Americans to refuse the American settlement of their native lands in the West.

Geronimo (far right) with three warriors, 1886

Prisoners of War (Geronimo is third from right)

Upon the surrender of Geronimo in 1886, the Apache Wars were virtually over, and the entire Chiricahua Apache tribe was evacuated from the Southwest and held as prisoners of war in Florida, Alabama, and Fort Sill, Oklahoma. With no leaders willing to assume Geronimo's campaign of resistance, the various Apache groups thought it in their best interest not to incur additional wrath from the U. S. government. For its part, rather than risk a resurgent uprising, the federal government thought it in their best interest not to amass all the Chiricahua Apache at Fort Sill until after Geronimo had died.

Chapter 6: Rebellion at Cibecue Creek

An Apache warrior by William F. Farny

"It is the general impression here that the men of the Indian scout company will go with their friends if they break out. Please give me authority to discharge them or such of them as I may believe unreliable and enlist reliable ones in their places." – Eugene Carr

While many people within and outside the Army doubted the Apaches could be made into loyal and reliable soldiers, the large majority of the scouts proved them wrong. There was only one large-scale mutiny, and that one led to tragic consequences both for the scouts and the cavalry.

On August 30, 1881, a column of troops headed out from Fort Apache led by General Eugene Carr. The column included 5 officers, 79 enlisted men of the 6th Cavalry, 9 civilians, and 23 Apache scouts, and the mission was to ride to nearby Cibecue Creek to bring a Cibecue Apache medicine man named Noch-ay-det-klinne in for questioning.

Carr

Noch-ay-det-klinne was an unusual figure. He had been part of the peace delegations that visited President Grant at the White House in 1871, and the following year he served as an Apache scout, though that didn't last long. He also got some education in a religious school in Santa Fe, but Noch-ay-det-klinne knew the white man and his ways and was thoroughly unimpressed. He returned home to become a medicine man and soon began to preach that he could raise the dead; in fact, he announced that he would raise some honored chiefs who had died in battles against the U.S. Cavalry. Apaches flocked in from the nearby San Carlos Reservation around to attend his all-night dances and ceremonies, and they lavished the medicine man with gifts. Even the Apache scouts from Fort Apache attended, and their white officers noted that once they returned, they were secretive about what they had heard and seen.

Rumors began to fly that Noch-ay-det-klinne was making other predictions, including that the white man would disappear from the land by harvest time. General Carr suspected this might be a call for an uprising, so he invited Noch-ay-det-klinne to come in to talk. When the medicine man ignored him, he decided to go get him.

General Carr worried about the loyalty of his scouts on such a sensitive mission, so he didn't tell them its purpose. Given the direction they headed, though, it soon became obvious. The day's march was uneventful and that evening at camp, the general explained the mission as he issued the scouts their weapons and ammunition. According to Apache reports, he also sarcastically asked if they planned to use them on whites or Apaches. The scouts protested that they were loyal, and Carr seems to have taken them at their word. Two scouts offered to go ahead and talk with Noch-ay-det-klinne, to which Carr agreed.

The next morning, as the column approached Noch-ay-det-klinne's village near Cibeque Creek, the soldiers began to grow suspicious. They came to a spot where the trail forked. Both paths led to the village, and the Apache scouts wanted to go on the longer trail because it followed the creek and provided a ready supply of water. When General Carr refused and told them to take the shorter route, the scouts seemed angry. Later the soldiers agreed the scouts had probably planned an ambush there.

While the soldiers' suspicions weren't raised by this except in retrospect, they did feel unsettled as Apache villagers appeared out of the brush along the trail in small groups and began following them to the village. Soon they had quite a large number following them, and others going ahead. One Apache known to them, a man named Sanchez, rode the length of the column and appeared to be counting the troops. When questioned, he said he was going home, but the soldiers realized he was heading in the wrong direction.

By midafternoon, the column reached Noch-ay-det-klinne's village, and from this point there are two versions of events. The Army's official report states that after some wrangling, General Carr convinced the medicine man to come along with the promise that he wouldn't try to escape. Apache accounts say the soldiers began abusing the villagers and rudely dragged the medicine man out of his wikiup. Carr provided an account of the meeting: "'I told him through the interpreter what I had come for, as I had told the scouts the night before. This was told him in the presence of the other Indians, in their own language, so all should understand. [There were only about three male Indians around, besides the scouts.] . . . I then told him I would treat him as a friend till those charges had been investigated and if not true he would be released. He had already denied them. He showed me a pass from the Agent for himself and others to plant corn on Cibicu for 60 days, dated May 13th, and extended July 13th for another 60 days. I told him the Agent wanted me to bring him in to talk & etc. He made [an] excuse for not coming before, that he had a patient to attend, and the Indians would have blamed him if he had left the sick man; but said he had cured him, and he had gone home this morning and he, Nock-ay-det-klinne, was now ready to go with me. I told him that was all right and if it was all explained he would be released in a few days. I then ordered a guard detailed [one noncommissioned officer and eight men]; told him who was In charge of that, Sergeant [John E] McDonald, Troop E, 6th Cavalry; that if he tried to escape he would be killed. He smiled and said he did not want to escape, he was perfectly willing to go. I then told him that if there were an attempt at rescue he would be killed. He smiled at that also, and said no one would attempt to rescue him. I also told him he could take part of his family along with him. This talk was all in the presence of other Indians, purposely to reassure them and make a good case to their minds. Mose at times repeated and explained, when he did not seem to catch the meaning of Interpreter Hurrle. I thought that the possession of his person, as a hostage, would make them particularly careful not to bring on a collision."

The column headed out with no trouble, and General Carr led about half the men ahead, thinking the other half accompanying Noch-ay-det-klinne were right behind him. In fact, the medicine man had delayed leaving, and now that half of the column was lagging behind. General Carr did not seem concerned when he found out about this and continued towards the creek. Since the sun was already sloping to the west, he decided only to march a couple of miles from the village and camp beside Cibecue Creek.

It proved to be a fatal decision. The soldiers made camp on an open little mesa overlooking the creek, and as they did so, they spotted a hundred or more Apaches gathering near the stream, stripped down to their breechclouts and moccasins as if ready for battle. Almost all carried rifles, while a few had bows. An Apache scout, Sergeant Dandy Jim, was with them. When one of the cavalry officers ordered them to go away, they ignored him.

Meanwhile, the Apache scouts were setting up camp at a spot where they had been ordered to next to the soldiers' camp. They protested that there were too many ants in the spot and asked to move. When this request was granted, they moved closer to the gathering Apaches.

Despite these suspicious moves, the soldiers continued to unpack their belongings and prepare supper. Just then, one of the village Apaches, who had ridden into the soldiers' camp, began to wave his rifle over his head and shout to his fellow tribesmen. Several villagers fired, and an instant later the Apache scouts let off a volley right into the unsuspecting cavalrymen. Several went down instantly, and as the remaining soldiers dove for whatever cover they could find, the scouts and villagers hid under the edge of the mesa. After a few parting shots, they retreated across the creek and took up positions behind rocks and underbrush and atop a nearby hill. As they went, they made short work of three soldiers watering some of the column's horses at the creek.

After that, the Apaches started firing in earnest, and the hail of bullets was so bad the soldiers had to keep covered and could barely fire any answering shots. Luckily, the second half of the column with Noch-ay-det-klinne appeared, and Carr immediately sent them on a charge to clear out the closest Apaches hiding in the underbrush along the creek. This got rid of the most accurate fire, but the Apaches continued to shoot at the troops exposed on the mesa. General Carr later reported that about 60 Apaches, including some of the scouts, had fired at them first, but at this point of the battle some 200 Apaches, both scouts and villagers, were firing on his position.

If their object was to save their medicine man, they had badly miscalculated, because Carr had ordered Noch-ay-det-klinne's guards to kill him if there was any trouble. As bullets flew in both directions, Noch-ay-det-klinne tried to crawl away. A sergeant shot him through both legs, and the column's trumpeter hurried up to finish him off with a shot through the head.

Carr spread out his men to all sides in case the Apaches tried a sneak attack, but none ever came. The Apaches continued to snipe from their positions until nightfall ended the battle. Under cover of darkness, Carr ordered his men to pack up what they could and move out. Almost half of their mounts had been killed in the crossfire, and many supplies had to be left behind. In order for them not to fall into Apache hands, he ordered them destroyed.

As they were preparing to leave, one of the men checked on Noch-ay-det-klinne's body and to his astonishment found him still breathing. He was killed for good with a harsh blow of an axe to his skull.

Noch-ay-det-klinne was the only confirmed casualty on the Apache side. Seven soldiers had been killed and two wounded, mostly from the initial volley fired at point blank range. The soldiers quietly buried those dead they could find and slipped away back towards Fort Apache.

They got back without any more fighting, but the countryside had erupted in chaos. Renegade Apaches raided farms and ranches and killed dozens of settlers, as well as a few isolated soldiers. They even attacked Fort Apache itself on September 1, something the Apaches never did before or since. Once again, the Apaches spared themselves heavy losses and didn't make a direct assault, contenting themselves to snipe at long range on the fort for several hours and wounding three soldiers.

In response, the army mobilized thousands of troops to deal with the trouble and crisscrossed the desert with numerous columns. There were several skirmishes, the biggest being on July 17, 1882 at Big Dry Wash (also called Big Dry Fork), where the main group of renegades fought a desperate rearguard action, losing 16 men, including two former Apache scouts, before the rest made their escape. These heavy losses pacified all but the most hardcore Apache; most snuck back to the reservation, others turned themselves in to the authorities, and those who were still defiant fled to Mexico. On March 3 of that year, three scouts - Dead Shot, Dandy Jim, and Skippy - were hanged for treason at Fort Grant. Many soldiers disagreed with this treatment, saying that most Apache scouts did not fire during the initial volleys and only joined the fighting when the soldiers started shooting at any Apache in sight.

General Crook was brought back in to take over command in Arizona in September, and he had a long talk with many of the Apache involved, both villagers and scouts. They all insisted that Americans opened fire first. This was an unusual development, although it might be explained that the presence of so many armed Apache made the man, who was probably a civilian contractor, get jumpy. They also said that the soldiers had trampled the village cornfield and hit some of the villagers. Crook wrote in his report, "The Indians are so firmly of the belief that the affair of the Cibeque last year was an attack premeditated by the white soldiers, that I am convinced any attempt to punish one of the Indian soldiers for participation in it would bring on a war. Without wishing to express an opinion on that affair, I have no doubt from what I know of the Indians and the country in question that, if the Indians had been in earnest, not one of our soldiers could have gotten away from there alive. Of course, afterwards, it was perfectly natural for the Indians who had lost friends and relations, to commit the depredations, which they did in the vicinity of Fort Apache."

Whatever the truth of the matter, it left a serious stain on the reputation of the Apache Scouts.

Chapter 7: The Apache Kid

The Apache Kid

While the Battle at Cibecue Creek has been all but forgotten, another renegade scout has become an enduring legend of the Wild West. In the late 1870s in the northern Arizona mining town of Globe, there was a local figure named Haskay-bay-nay-natyl, which in Apache means "the tall man destined to come to a mysterious end." Residents of Globe couldn't pronounce that, so they simply called him the Apache Kid. He had been born in the San Carlos reservation in the 1860s and was probably from the White Mountain Apache people, but details of his early life are vague.

The Apache Kid worked various jobs around Globe, showing no inclination to live on the reservation. His work in Globe had given him a good command of the English language and the ability to move easily between two vastly different cultures. He was well-liked and soon caught the eye of Al Sieber, a German who had immigrated to America at a young age, fought for the Union in the Civil War, and moved to Arizona to become a prospector. In 1871, Sieber found a job as an Army scout and proved himself invaluable. Like the best military men on the frontier, he respected Native American cultures and tried to learn as much as he could about them. This, however, did not stop him from fighting renegade Apaches, and by the time of his death in 1907, his body bore 28 bullet wounds, one of which was from the Apache Kid.

Sieber

Of course, that was all in the future. Sieber was a young scout on the rise, and in the even younger Apache Kid he saw a likely assistant. In fact, he saw his flipside: an Apache who was proud to be Apache but still understood and respected the white man's ways. Sieber recruited him as a scout well before Crook decided to experiment with Apache Scouts on a larger and more organized scale.

The Apache Kid (in the center) as a scout for the Americans

Little is known about those early years, but in 1881 the Apache Kid officially joined Crook's band of scouts under Sieber's recommendation. He proved Sieber's hunch was right and in July 1882 was promoted to sergeant. His first years in the scouts were eventful ones, since there were many renegades to track, and in 1883 he went with Crook on his expedition to hunt renegades in the Sierra Madre in Mexico.

1885 found him back in Mexico with Sieber, now Chief of Scouts, hunting Geronimo. He went back later in the year with the famous Indian fighter Lieutenant Emmet Crawford, but this time things didn't go so well. The Apache Kid had a fondness for liquor, and like many a man before him this fondness got him into trouble. In the town of Huasabas, Sonora, he and a group of other scouts got drunk on the local booze and ended up rioting. The Mexicans feared the Apache when they were sober, and they were downright terrified of them when they were drunk. Soon he and his fellow revelers were in the Huasabas jailhouse, facing the possibility of a firing squad.

Crawford

Luckily, cooler heads prevailed. The U.S. Army was trying to stamp out renegade Apaches in Mexico, and the judge decided not to start an international incident by executing its scouts. The Apache Kid got off with a $20 fine and the Army sent him back to the San Carlos Reservation. He had kept his life, but his Army career had been tarnished.

Nonetheless, he continued to serve in the scouts, where his language ability, marksmanship, and knack for tracking renegades made him highly valuable. In May 1887, he was left in command of the scouts and guardhouse at the San Carlos Reservation while Al Sieber and the local commander, Captain Francis Pierce, were away. That was a mistake, because the Huasabas affair hadn't dried up the Apache Kid's thirst for alcohol and he participated in a *tiswin* party, where the men got together to brew corn liquor and drink until they were stupefied. It was illegal on the reservation and the Apache Kid was supposed to enforce the law in Pierce's absence. Nevertheless, he drank with the rest of them.

Soon the Apaches got into a drunken brawl with each other that escalated to gunplay, and a warrior named Gon-Zizzie killed the Apache Kid's father, Togo-de-Chuz. In retaliation, the Apache Kid's friends killed Gon-Zizzie. Still burning for revenge, the Kid hunted down Gon-Zizzie's brother Rip and killed him too. The Kid and four other scouts involved in the fight fled the reservation, only to return to face the music a month later. They were ordered to give up their weapons, which they did, and as they were being led to the guardhouse, followed by a large crowd, a shot rang out, then several more. Sieber was wounded in the leg.

The Apache Kid and the other scouts fled with the Fourth Cavalry hot on their trail, but the cavalry caught up with the renegade scouts and surprised them in their camp in the Rincon Mountains. While the scouts managed to get away, they had to leave their horses and all their equipment behind. Being without a mount or supplies would be a slow death for the average American, but the Apaches were accustomed to such hardships and continued their life on the run. The Kid wanted to return, however, and sent a message to General Miles offering to turn himself in if he got a fair trial. This was granted, and the Kid and the other scouts involved in the drunken gunfight found themselves before a judge.

The judge sentenced them to be executed by a firing squad. General Miles pled on their behalf, and the sentence was reduced to life in prison. Miles then managed to get that reduced down to 10 years. The prisoners were sent to Alcatraz, but in 1888 they returned to San Carlos, having been pardoned because the judge was found to have been prejudiced against them.

The Apache Kid while being held prisoner

As it turned out, their freedom didn't last long. The local white community was angered that they had gotten off so easily and had a judge retry them for the prison break and the wounding of Sieber, even though the scouts had all been disarmed at the time. On October 25, 1889, the Apache Kid and three other scouts were found guilty and got seven years in Yuma Territorial Prison.

As the prison wagon headed to Yuma filled with the Apaches and several other convicts, the prisoners made a desperate break. They killed one guard, and another seems to have died of a heart attack, perhaps from fear of being at the mercy of the Apaches. The third guard was badly beaten up but allowed to live. He later testified that the prisoners wanted to crush his head with a rock but the Apache Kid stopped them.

As the prisoners ran off, a snowstorm swept over the land, hiding their tracks. The Apache Kid was never seen again, or at least, no sighting was ever confirmed. He was said to have created a band of renegade Apaches who hid out in Mexico's Sierra Madre. From there, they launched raids on ranchers and farmers in northern Mexico, Arizona, and New Mexico. Some Apaches tell the tale that he actually did these raids alone because he had been rejected by his own people. The Apache Kid, they said, had become a ruthless killer, gunning men down for their cattle when he could have just as easily slipped away with them under the cover of darkness. They also say that he kidnapped Apache women to be his unwilling wives, a terrible crime in a culture that held female chastity in high regard. He was even said to have killed them when he got bored with them and then went hunting for another one.

One of these wives reappeared one day saying she had escaped her captor because he was dying of tuberculosis in the Sierra Madre. The date for this tale is various given as 1894 and 1910, so it must be looked upon with suspicion. There are many other stories of his death in the United States or Mexico. One has even been accepted officially. In the Apache Kid Wilderness in the Cibola National Forest, there is a monument on Blue Mountain that claims a group of ranchers tracked him down after one of raids and killed him in 1906. Some Apache sources say this was in fact another warrior named Massai.

Even as late as the 1920s, ranchers in Arizona and Sonora complained about Apache rustling their cattle and whispered that the Apache Kid, who had long passed from being a kid into ripe yet defiant old age, was behind the thefts. With no evidence to the contrary, it was easy for people to believe this ghost from a different era was still out there in the desert somewhere.

Thus the Apache Kid passed into legend, becoming one of the many Wild West figures, like Jesse James and Butch Cassidy, who seemingly cheated their own mortality and were never believed to actually be dead.

Chapter 8: The Final Era

Once General Miles had finally gotten the last renegades under Geronimo to surrender, the government decided that the best way to prevent further breakouts was to send the Chiricahua Apaches and some of the other diehards to Florida as prisoners of war. In 1886, they were packed into railway cars and shipped far away from their homeland. Going with them were the Chiricahua Apache scouts, not as guards but as deportees. Many officers protested at this lack of gratitude for men who had fought hard for the United States, but the government remained unmoved. Thus, for 26 years, some of the best Apache scouts were held as prisoners of war with the same renegade Apaches they helped capture. After a time many of the prisoners were moved to Oklahoma and were allowed to farm, but the vast majority, including the scouts, never saw their homeland again. Other bands of Apaches were never deported and remained on the San Carlos Reservation, where they live to this day.

The removal of the Chiricahua didn't end the era of Apache scouts but only limited their number. In fact, a few managed to stay on and performed good service. In 1891, the number of Native American scouts was cut because the end of the Geronimo campaign meant there was less need for them; that year, Congress dictated that only 50 should be assigned to Arizona and 150 nationwide. Most of those in Arizona and New Mexico, of course, were Apache.

Those few remaining Apache scouts were used to maintain forts, patrol the border, and hunt after deserters. In 1916, a contingent of 39 Apache scouts joined General Pershing on his campaign to hunt Pancho Villa in Mexico. While the Mexican government kicked the soldiers out before they could catch the Mexican revolutionary, the Apache scouts proved their worth once again. Captain James A. Shannon recalled, "The Indian cannot be beaten at his own game. But in order to get results, he must be allowed to play that game in his own way. You tell a troop of white soldiers there is an enemy a thousand yards in your front and they will go straight at him without questions. The Indian under the same circumstance wants to look it all over first. He wants to go to one side and take a look. Then to the other side and take a look. He is like a wild animal stalking its prey. Before he advances he wants to know just what is in his front. This extreme caution, which we don't like to see in the white man, is one of the qualities that makes him a perfect scout. It would be al- most impossible to surprise an outfit that had a detachment of Apache scouts in its front. They do not lack courage by any means. They have taken part in some little affairs in Mexico that required plenty of courage, but they must be allowed to do things in their own way." Shannon also noted that the age-old Apache hatred of Mexicans almost led to trouble on a number of occasions, and their white officers had to keep an eye on them in case they shot friendly Mexicans along with the hostile ones.

After that campaign, the scouts were required to sign on for a seven-year term like other soldiers. Previously they could sign on for three months, six months, or a whole year. With their dwindling numbers, they were being brought more into the fold of regular army regulations. Their separate units, which had existed since 1866, were discontinued in 1921, even though they still performed separate service from the rank and file. To recognize this, they were put on the Detached Enlisted Men's List.

Apache scouts in 1919

The last four Apache scouts, now well into middle age, retired in 1947. One of them was Sergeant Sinew Riley, son of Apache scout John Riley and grandson of Apache scout Dead Shot, one of the original recruits by Crook in 1871 and one of the three scouts hanged for the Cibecue Creek affair. Sinew Riley was proud of his family's three generations of service and always maintained his grandfather's innocence. In his retirement speech, Riley said, "We were recruited from the warriors of many famous nations. We are the last of the Army's Indian Scouts. In a few years we shall have gone to join our comrades…beyond the sunset, for our need here is no more. There we shall always remain very proud of our Indian people and of the United States Army, for we were truly the first Americans and you in the Army are now our warriors." Sinew Riley died in 1960, still loyal to the nation.

Riley

The last surviving Apache scout was Sergeant Julius Colelay, who died in 1988 at the age of 90, having lived into an era where the origins of the Apache scouts were already enshrined in history.

Online Resources

Other books about Native American tribes by Charles River Editors

Bibliography

Ball, Eve, "The Apache Scouts: A Chiricahua Appraisal" in *Arizona and the West*, Vol. 7, No. 4 (Winter 1965)

Ball, Eve, *In the Days of Victorio: Recollections of a Warm Springs Apache* (University of Arizona Press, Tucson, 1970)

Ball, Eve, with Nora Henn and Lynda Sanchez, *Indeh: An Apache Odyssey* (Brigham Young University Press, Provo, Utah, 1980)

Basso, Keith (editor) from the notes of Grenville Goodwin, *Western Apache Raiding and Warfare* (University of Arizona Press, Tucson, 1971)

Betzinez, Jason, with Wilber Sturtevant Nye, *I Fought with Geronimo* (The Stackpole Company, New York, 1959)

Chamberlain, Kathleen, *Victorio: Apache Warrior and Chief* (University of Oklahoma Press, Norman, 2007)

Colwell-Chanthaphonh, Chip, "Western Apache Oral Histories and Traditions of the Camp Grant Massacre" in *The American Indian Quarterly*, Volume 27, Number 3&4, Summer/Fall 2003

Crook, George, *General George Crook: His Autobiography* (University of Oklahoma Press, Norman, 1946)

Dunlay, Tom, *Kit Carson & The Indians* (University of Nebraska Press, Lincoln, 2000)

Geronimo, with S.M. Barrett, ed., *Geronimo: His Own Story* (Ballantine Books, New York, 1971)

Johnson, David, *Final report on the Battle of Cieneguilla : a Jicarilla Apache victory over the U.S. Dragoons, March 30, 1854* (U.S. Dept. of Agriculture, Forest Service, Southwestern Region, Archaeological Report Series No. 20, Albuquerque, 2009)

Pettis, George Henry, *Kit Carson's Fight with the Comanche and Kiowa Indians at the Adobe Walls* (Providence: Rider, 1878; rpt., Santa Fe, 1908)

Radbourne, Allan, "The Battle for Apache Pass: Reports of the California Volunteers" in *The Brand Book*, Vol. 34, No. 2, Spring 2001 (The English Westerners Society, London, 2001)

Rajtar, Steve, *Indian War Sites: A Guidebook to Battlefields, Monuments, and Memorials* (McFarland & Company, Inc., Jefferson, North Carolina, 1999)

Secoy, Frank, *Changing Military Patterns on the Great Plains* (American Ethnological Society, Monograph No. 21, J. J. Augustin, Locust Valley, NY, 1953)

Stevens, Robert, "The Apache Menace in Sonora, 1831-1849", in *Arizona and the West*, Vol. 6, No. 3, Autumn 1964

Thrapp, Dan, *The Conquest of Apacheria* (University of Oklahoma Press, Norman, 1975)

Utley, Robert, Frontier Regulars: *The United States Army and the Indian, 1866-1891* (Macmillan Publishing Company, New York, 1973)

Walker, Harry, "Soldier in the California Column: The Diary of John W. Teal", in *Arizona and the West*, Vol. 13, No. 1, Spring 1971

Williams, Jack, and Robert Hoover, *Arms of the Apacheria: A Comparison of Apachean and Spanish Fighting Techniques in the later 18th Century*. Katunob: Occasional Publications in Mesoamerican Anthropology, No. 25. (University of Northern Colorado, Greeley, 1983)

CPSIA information can be obtained
at www.ICGtesting.com
Printed in the USA
LVHW021604270423
745406LV00007B/448